REALLY EASY GUITAR

ACOUSTIC SONGS

22 SONGS WITH CHORDS, LYRICS & BASIC TAB

ISBN 978-1-5400-4062-6

Visit Hal Leonard Online at
www.halleonard.com

Contact us:
Hal Leonard
7777 West Bluemound Road
Milwaukee, WI 53213
Email: info@halleonard.com

In Europe, contact:
Hal Leonard Europe Limited
42 Wigmore Street
Marylebone, London, W1U 2RN
Email: info@halleonardeurope.com

In Australia, contact:
Hal Leonard Australia Pty. Ltd.
4 Lentara Court
Cheltenham, Victoria, 3192 Australia
Email: info@halleonard.com.au

GUITAR NOTATION LEGEND

Chord Diagrams

CHORD DIAGRAMS graphically represent the guitar fretboard to show correct chord fingerings.

- The letter above the diagram tells the name of the chord.
- The top, bold horizontal line represents the nut of the guitar. Each thin horizontal line represents a fret. Each vertical line represents a string; the low E string is on the far left and the high E string is on the far right.
- A dot shows where to put your fret-hand finger and the number at the bottom of the diagram tells which finger to use.
- The "O" above the string means play it open, while an "X" means don't play the string.

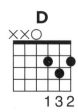

Tablature

TABLATURE graphically represents the guitar fingerboard. Each horizontal line represents a string, and each number represents a fret.

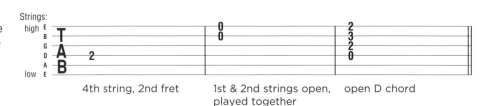

4th string, 2nd fret   1st & 2nd strings open, played together   open D chord

Definitions for Special Guitar Notation

HAMMER-ON: Strike the first (lower) note with one finger, then sound the higher note (on the same string) with another finger by fretting it without picking.

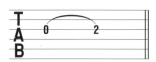

PULL-OFF: Place both fingers on the notes to be sounded. Strike the first note and without picking, pull the finger off to sound the second (lower) note.

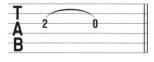

LEGATO SLIDE: Strike the first note and then slide the same fret-hand finger up or down to the second note. The second note is not struck.

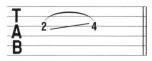

SHIFT SLIDE: Same as legato slide, except the second note is struck.

Additional Musical Definitions

N.C. • No chord. Instrument is silent.

 • Repeat measures between signs.

Every Rose Has Its Thorn

Words and Music by Bobby Dall, C.C. Deville, Bret Michaels and Rikki Rockett

 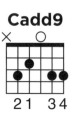  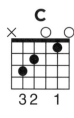 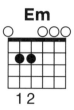 

INTRO

Slow

| G | Cadd9 | G | Cadd9 ||

VERSE 1

G   **Cadd9**
We both lie silent and still in the dead of the night. Although we

G   **Cadd9**
both lie close together, we feel miles apart inside. Was it

G   **Cadd9**   **G**   **Cadd9**
somethin' I said or somethin' I did? Did my words not come out right? Though I

D   **C**
tried not to hurt you, though I tried. But I guess that's why they say

CHORUS 1

G   **Cadd9**   **G**   **Cadd9**
every rose has its thorn, just like every night has its dawn. Just like

G   **D**   **Cadd9**   **G**   **Cadd9**
every cowboy sings a sad, sad song, every rose has its thorn.

REPEAT INTRO

VERSE 2

G   **Cadd9**
I listen to our favorite song playin' on the radio. Hear the

G   **Cadd9**
DJ say love's a game of easy come and   easy go. But I

G   **Cadd9**   **G**   **Cadd9**
wonder, does he know? Has he ever felt like this? And I

D   **C**
know that you'd be here right now if I   coulda let you know somehow. I guess

REPEAT CHORUS 1

BRIDGE

Em	D	Cadd9	G	G5/F#

Though it's been a while now, I can still feel so much pain.

Em	D	C

Like the knife that cuts you, the wound heals,   but the scar, that scar remains.

REPEAT INTRO

VERSE 3

G		Cadd9

I know I coulda saved a love that night if I'd   known what to say.

G		Cadd9

'Stead of makin' love, we both   made our separate ways. And now I

G	Cadd9	G	Cadd9

hear you found somebody new and that I never meant that much to you. To

D	C

hear that tears me up inside and to see you cuts me like a knife. I guess

CHORUS 2

G	Cadd9	G	Cadd9

every rose has its thorn, just like every night has its dawn. Just like

G	D	Cadd9	G

every cowboy sings a sad, sad song, every rose has its

thorn.

Free Fallin'

Words and Music by Tom Petty and Jeff Lynne

(Capo 1st Fret)

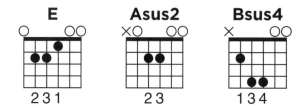

INTRO

Moderately slow

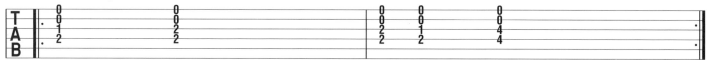

VERSE 1

	E	Asus2	E	Bsus4		E	Asus2		E	Bsus4

She's a good girl, loves   her mama, loves Je - sus and America   too.

	E	Asus2	E	Bsus4		E	Asus2		E	Bsus4

She's a good girl,   crazy 'bout Elvis, loves hors - es and her boyfriend too.

REPEAT INTRO (1 TIME)

VERSE 2

	E	Asus2	E	Bsus4		E	Asus2		E	Bsus4

And it's a long day livin' in   Reseda. There's a free - way runnin' through the yard.

	E	Asus2		E	Bsus4		E	Asus2		E	Bsus4

And I'm a bad boy 'cause I don't even miss her. I'm a bad boy for breakin' her heart. And I'm

CHORUS

E	Asus2		E	Bsus4		E	Asus2		E	Bsus4	
free,					free	fall - in'.				Yeah, I'm

E	Asus2		E	Bsus4		E	Asus2		E	Bsus4	
free,					free	fall - in'.				

VERSE 3

	E	Asus2	E	Bsus4		E	Asus2		E	Bsus4

Now all the vam - pires walkin' through the valley move west down Ventura Boulevard. And all the

E	Asus2		E	Bsus4		E	Asus2		E	Bsus4

bad boys are standin' in the shadows. And the good girls are home with broken hearts. Now I'm

REPEAT CHORUS

REPEAT INTRO (4 TIMES)

VERSE 4

        E   Asus2   E   Bsus4   E   Asus2   E   Bsus4
I wanna glide down   over Mulholland, I wanna write her name in the sky.

        E   Asus2   E   Bsus4   E   Asus2   E   Bsus4
I'm gonna free fall   out into nothin', gonna leave this world for a while. Now I'm

REPEAT CHORUS

INTERLUDE

Yeah, I'm

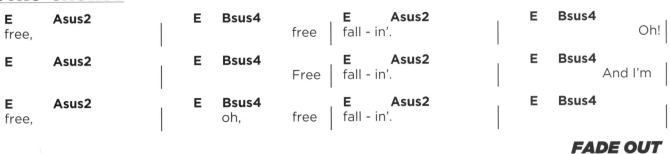

OUTRO-CHORUS

E Asus2		E Bsus4		E Asus2		E Bsus4
free,			free	fall - in'.		Oh!
E Asus2		E Bsus4		E Asus2		E Bsus4
			Free	fall - in'.		And I'm
E Asus2		E Bsus4		E Asus2		E Bsus4
free,		oh,	free	fall - in'.		

FADE OUT

E Asus2		E Bsus4		E Asus2	
			Free	fall - in'.	

Good Riddance
(Time of Your Life)

Words by Billie Joe
Music by Green Day

G
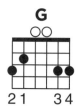

Cadd9
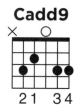

D
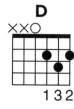

Em

INTRO

Very fast

‖: G | | Cadd9 | D :‖

VERSE 1

G   Cadd9   D
Another turnin' point, a fork stuck in the road.

G   Cadd9   D
Time grabs you by the wrist, directs you where to go.

Em   D   Cadd9   G
So make the best of this test, and don't ask why.

Em   D   Cadd9   G
It's not a question but a lesson learned in time.

CHORUS

Em   G   Em   G
It's something unpredictable but in the end is right.

Em   D
I hope you had the time of your life.

REPEAT INTRO (2 TIMES)

VERSE 2

G   Cadd9   D
So take the photographs and still-frames in your mind.

G   Cadd9   D
Hang it on a shelf in good health and good time.

Em   D   Cadd9   G
Tattoos of memories and dead skin on trial.

Em   D   Cadd9   G
For what it's worth, it was worth all the while.

REPEAT CHORUS

INTERLUDE

Play 4 times

‖: G | | Cadd9 | D :‖

‖: Em | D | Cadd9 | G :‖

REPEAT CHORUS

REPEAT INTRO (2 TIMES)

REPEAT CHORUS

OUTRO

‖: G | | Cadd9 | D :‖ G | ‖

Half of My Heart

Words and Music by John Mayer

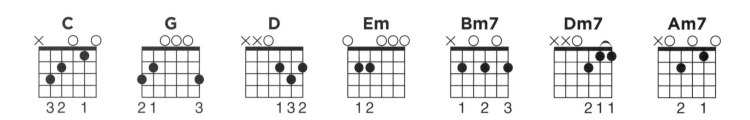

INTRO

Moderately

| C | G | | D | Em | C | G | | D | | | |

| C | G | | D | Em | C | | | | |

VERSE 1

C   G   D   Em   C   G   D
I was born in the arms of imaginary   friends,

C   G   D   Em   C   G   D
Free to roam, made a home out of everywhere I've   been.

C   G   D   Em
Then   you come crashin' in like the realest thing.

C   G   D
Try'n'   my best to understand all that you love can bring.

CHORUS 1

C   G   D   Em   C   G   D
Oh, half of my heart's got a grip on the situation. Half of my heart takes time.

C   G   D   Em   C   D
Half of my heart's got a right mind to tell you that I can't keep lovin' you, oh, with half of my heart.

INTERLUDE 1

| G | D | | Em | C | G | D | | Em | C | |

VERSE 2

```
C        G         D          Em        C       G       D
    I was made to believe I'd never love somebody else.

C        G         D          Em        C       G       D
    Made a plan, stay the man who can only love himself.

      C           G         D     Em
Lone - ly was the song I sang till the day you came,

           C          G             D
and show - in' me another way and all that my love can bring.
```

REPEAT CHORUS 1

INTERLUDE 2

```
G               D       | Em        C      | G          D        | Em      C            ||
                        | With half of my heart. |
```

BRIDGE

```
    G    Bm7       Dm7            Am7
Your faith is strong, but I can only fall short for so long.

       G       Bm7      Dm7             Am7
Down the road, later on, you will hate that I never gave more to you than

C                  D
half of my heart, but I can't stop lovin' you.

    C                  D                   N.C.
I can't stop lovin' you. I can't stop lovin' you with half of my,

C      G      D     Em      C      G      D
half of my heart,          oh, half of my heart.
```

CHORUS 2

```
C        G         D          Em        C       G         D
Half of my heart's got a real good imagination. Half of my heart's got you.

C        G         D          Em        C       G         D
Half of my heart's got a right mind to tell you that half of my heart won't do.

C        G        D     Em         C       G         D
Half of my heart is a shotgun wedding to a bride with a paper ring.

      C       G        D      Em          C       G        D
And half of my heart is the part of a man who's never truly loved anything.
```

OUTRO (REPEAT AND FADE)

```
C        G       D      Em        C       G       D
Half of my heart,          oh, half of my heart.
```

Hallelujah

Words and Music by Leonard Cohen

(Capo 5th Fret)

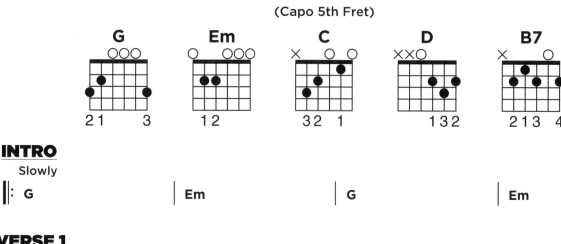

INTRO

Slowly

‖: G | Em | G | Em :‖

VERSE 1

```
        G              Em            G                Em
Well, I heard there was a secret chord that David played, and it pleased the Lord,

        C            D           G            D
but you don't really care for music, do ya?

        G                C         D        Em                C
Well, it goes like this: the fourth, the fifth, the minor fall, and the major lift.

        D              B7          Em
The baffled king composing, "Hallelujah."
```

CHORUS 1

```
        C          Em        C       G  D G       Em      G      Em
Hallelujah, hallelujah, hallelujah, halelu  -  jah.
```

VERSE 2

```
        G                        Em                 G                Em
Well, your faith was strong, but you needed proof. You saw her bathing on the roof.

        C            D           G            D
Her beauty and the moonlight overthrew ya.

        G                C         D     Em                          C
As she tied you to her kitchen chair,     as she broke your throne and she cut your hair,

        D              B7          Em
and from your lips you drew the hallelujah.
```

REPEAT CHORUS 1

VERSE 3

```
        G              Em            G                  Em
Well, baby, I've been here before. I've seen this room, and I've walked this floor.

        C            D           G            D
You know, I used to live alone before I knew ya.
```

```
         G                  C    D    Em        C
And I've seen your flag on the marble arch, and love is not a victory march.

         D          B7        Em
It's a cold, and it's a broken hallelujah.
```

REPEAT CHORUS 1

VERSE 4

```
              G               Em           G          Em
Well, there was a time when you let me know what's really going on below,

   C              D    G          D
but now you never show that to me, do ya?

     G          C      D         Em          C
But remember when I moved in you, and the holy dove was moving too,

     D          B7         Em
and every breath we drew was hallelujah?
```

CHORUS 2

```
     C      Em      C      G  D
Hallelujah, hallelujah, hallelujah, halelu   -
```

INTERLUDE

```
C                    Em             C              G         D
jah.          |          |          |          |          |          |          ||
```

REPEAT INTRO (1 TIME)

VERSE 5

```
     G         Em         G          Em
Well, maybe there's a God above, but all I've ever learned from love

   C           D          G          D
was how to shoot somebody who outdrew ya.

     G          C    D      Em            C
And it's not a cry that you hear at night. It's not somebody who's seen the light.

     D          B7        Em
It's a cold, and it's a broken hallelujah.
```

REPEAT CHORUS 2 (2 TIMES)

OUTRO-CHORUS

```
     C      Em      C      G  D  G
Hallelujah, hallelujah, hallelujah, halelu   -   jah.
```

Hey, Soul Sister

Words and Music by Pat Monahan, Espen Lind and Amund Bjorklund

(Capo 9th Fret)

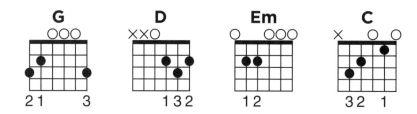

INTRO

Moderately

G		D		Em		C	
	Hey,		hey,		hey.		

VERSE 1

G   D   Em   C
Your lipstick stains on the front lobe of my left-side brains. I knew I wouldn't

G   D   Em   C   D
forget ya, and so I went and let you blow my mind.

G   D   Em   C
Your sweet moonbeam, the smell of you in every single dream I dream. I knew when we

G   D   Em   C   D
collided, you're the one I have decided who's one of my kind.

CHORUS 1

C   D   G D C   D   G D
Hey, soul sister, ain't that Mister Mister on the radio, stereo? The way you move ain't fair, you know.

C   D   G D C   D
Hey, soul sister, I don't wanna miss a single thing you do tonight.

REPEAT INTRO

VERSE 2

G   D   Em   C
Just in time, I'm so glad you have a one-track mind like me. You gave my life

G   D   Em   C   D
direction, a game-show love connection we can't deny.

G   D   Em   C
I'm so obsessed. My heart is bound to beat right out my untrimmed chest. I believe in

G   D   Em   C   D
you. Like a virgin, you're Madonna, and I'm always gonna wanna blow your mind.

REPEAT CHORUS 1

BRIDGE

G   D
  The way you can cut a rug, watching you's the only drug I

Em   C
need. Some gangsta, I'm so thug. You're the only one I'm dreamin' of. You see,

G   D
  I can be myself now, finally.   In fact, there's nothin' I can't

Em   C   D
be. I want the world to see you'll be with   me.

CHORUS 2

C   D   G   D   C   D   G   D
Hey, soul sister, ain't   that Mister Mister on the radio, stereo? The way you move ain't fair, you know.

C   D   G   D   C   D   G   D
Hey, soul sister, I   don't wanna miss a single thing you do tonight.

C   D   G   D   C   D
Hey, soul sister, I   don't wanna miss a single thing you do   tonight.

OUTRO

‖:   G   D   Em   C   D   G
              Hey, | hey, | hey, | tonight. :‖   ‖

Hey There Delilah

Words and Music by Tom Higgenson

(Capo 2nd Fret)

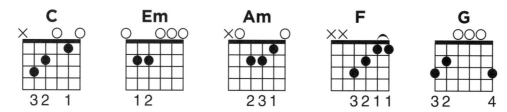

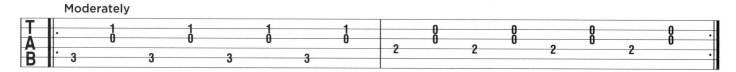

INTRO

Moderately

VERSE 1

C   Em
Hey there, Delilah, what's it like in New York City?

    C   Em   Am
I'm a thousand miles away, but girl, tonight you look so pretty. Yes you do.

F   G   Am   G
Times Square can't shine as bright as you. I swear it's true.

C   Em
Hey there, Delilah, don't you worry about the distance.

    C   Em   Am
I'm right there. If you get lonely, give this song another listen. Close your eyes,

F   G   Am   G
listen to my voice. It's my disguise. I'm by your side.

CHORUS 1

C   Am C   Am
Oh, it's what you do to me.   Oh, it's what you do to me.

C   Am C   Am   C
Oh, it's what you do to me.   Oh, it's what you do to me, what you do to me.

VERSE 2

C   Em
Hey there, Delilah, I know times are gettin' hard,

         C   Em   Am
but just believe me, girl, someday I'll pay the bills with this guitar. We'll have it good.

F   G   Am   G
We'll have the life we knew we would, my word is good.

```
C                              Em
     Hey there, Delilah, I've got so much left to say.

        C                              Em                        Am
If every simple song I wrote to you would take your breath away, I'd write it all.

F            G             Am            G
   Even more in love with me you'd    fall, we'd have it all.
```

CHORUS 2

```
C                 Am   C                 Am
Oh, it's what you do to me.   Oh, it's what you do to me.

C                 Am   C                 Am
Oh, it's what you do to me.   Oh, it's what you do to me.
```

BRIDGE

```
  F                          G
A thousand miles seems pretty far, but they've got planes and trains and cars.

     C                    Am
I'd walk to you if I had no other way.

  F                          G
Our friends would all make fun of us, and we'll just laugh along because

     C                    Am
we know that none of them have felt this way.

  F              G
Delilah, I can promise you that by the time that we get through,

  Am                              G
the world will never, ever be the same, and you're to blame.
```

VERSE 3

```
C                      Em
     Hey there, Delilah, you be good, and don't you miss me.

        C                          Em              Am
Two more years and you'll be done with school, and I'll be makin' history like I do.

F            G          Am     F        G         Am
   You'll know it's all because of you.    We can do whatever we want    to.

F            G          Am            G
   Hey there, Delilah, here's to you, this one's for you.
```

REPEAT CHORUS 1

OUTRO

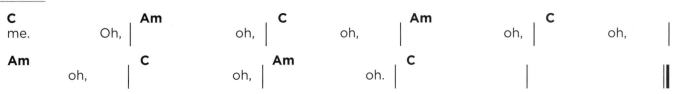

```
C                 Am              C              Am            C
me.        Oh,  |          oh,  |      oh,  |          oh,  |      oh,     |

Am              C              Am            C
      oh,  |          oh,  |      oh.  |                  |              ‖
```

Ho Hey

Words and Music by Jeremy Fraites and Wesley Schultz

C 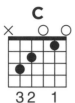 Csus4  Am 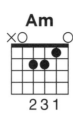 G 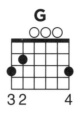 F  Gsus4

INTRO

Moderately slow

‖: **C** Ho! **Csus4** **C** Hey! **Csus4** :‖

VERSE 1

C I've been tryin' to do it right. **Csus4** **C** I've been livin' a lonely life. **Csus4**

C I've been sleepin' here instead. **Csus4** **C** I've been sleepin' in my bed.

Am I've been sleepin' in my bed. **G**

REPEAT INTRO (1 TIME)

VERSE 2

C So show me family, **Csus4** **C** all the blood that I will bleed. **Csus4**

C I don't know where I belong, **Csus4** **C** I don't know where I went wrong,

Am but I can write a song. **G** **C**

CHORUS 1

Am And I belong with you, **G** you belong with me. You're my sweet **C** - heart.

Am I belong with you, **G** you belong with me. You're my sweet...

VERSE 3

```
C                              Csus4   C                              Csus4
   I don't think you're right for him.    Look at what it might have been if you

C                              Csus4   C
   took a bus to Chinatown.              I'd be standin' on Canal

Am           G         C
   and Bowery.

Am                       G            C
   And she'd be standin' next to me.
```

CHORUS 2

```
              Am              G            C
   And I belong with you, you belong with me. You're my sweet - heart.

              Am              G            C
   I belong with you, you belong with me. You're my sweet - heart.
```

BRIDGE

```
F   C   Gsus4  C        F   C   Gsus4
Love, we    need it    now. Let's hope for    some. 'Cause

F   C   Gsus4  C
oh, we're bleedin' out.
```

OUTRO

```
C                        Csus4  | C                        Csus4
Ho!                             | Hey!

C                        Csus4  | C
Ho!                             | Hey!
```

I'm Yours

Words and Music by Jason Mraz

(Capo 4th Fret)

G 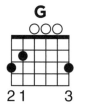 D  Em 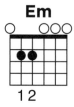 C 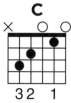 A7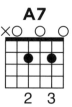

INTRO

Moderately slow

| G | | | D | | Em | | C | | |

VERSE 1

G
Well, a you done, done me in; you bet I felt it. I tried to be chill, but you're so hot that I melted. **D**

Em
I fell right through the cracks. Now I'm tryin' to get back. Before the **C**

G
cool done run out, I'll be givin' it my bestest, and nothin's gonna stop me but divine intervention. **D**

Em
I reckon it's again my turn to win some or learn some. **C**

CHORUS 1

G   **D**   **Em**   **C**
But I won't hesitate no more, no more. It cannot wait. I'm yours.

REPEAT INTRO

VERSE 2

G
Well, open up your mind, and see like me. Open up your plans and, damn, you're **D**

Em
free. Look into your heart, and you'll find love, love, love, love. **C**

G
Listen to the music of the moment. People dance and sing. We're just one big **D**

Em
family, and it's our god-forsaken right to be loved, loved, loved, loved, loved. **C**   **A7**

CHORUS 2

G   D   Em   C
So I won't hesitate no more, no more. It cannot wait. I'm sure there's no

G   D   Em   C
need to complicate. Our time is short. This is our fate. I'm yours.

INTERLUDE

G   D | Em   D
                                                              Scooch on over |

C   A7
closer, dear,   and I will nibble your | ear. |

G   D | Em   D | C | A7   N.C.   ‖

VERSE 3

                    G
I've been spendin' way too long checkin' my tongue in the mirror

      D
and bendin' over backwards just to try to see it clearer.

      Em   C
But my breath fogged up the glass, and so I drew a new face, and I laughed.

    G
I guess what I'll be sayin' is there ain't no better reason

     D
to rid yourself of vanities and just go with the seasons. It's

Em   C
what we aim to do. Our name is our virtue.

REPEAT CHORUS 1

VERSE 4

G   D
     Well, open up your mind and see like me. Open up your plans and, damn, you're

Em   C
free. Look into your heart, and you'll find that   the sky is yours.

    G   D
So please don't, please don't, please don't... There's no need to complicate 'cause our

Em   C   A7
time is short. This, ooh, this, ooh, this is our fate. I'm yours.

Iris

from the Motion Picture CITY OF ANGELS
Words and Music by John Rzeznik

Bm7 **Gmaj7**  **D5**  **D5/E** 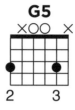 **G5** 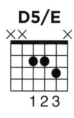 **Asus4** 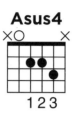 **Bm7/C#**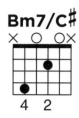

INTRO

Moderately

‖: Bm7 | | Gmaj7 | :‖

VERSE 1

D5   D5/E G5   Bm7   Asus4   G5
And I'd give up forever to touch you 'cause I know that you feel me somehow.

D5   D5/E   G5   Bm7   Asus4   G5
You're the closest to heaven that I'll ever be, and I don't wannna go home right now.

D5   D5/E   G5   Bm7 Asus4   G5
And all I could taste is this moment, and all I can breathe is your life.

D5   D5/E   G5   Bm7   Asus4   G5
And sooner or later it's over. I just don't wanna miss you tonight.

CHORUS

Bm7   Asus4   G5   Bm7   Asus4   G5
And I don't want the world to see me 'cause I don't think that they'd understand.

Bm7   Asus4   G5   Bm7   Asus4   G5
When everything's made to be broken, I just want you to know who I am.

REPEAT INTRO (2 TIMES)

VERSE 2

D5   D5/E   G5   Bm7   Asus4   G5
And you can't fight the tears that ain't comin' or the moment of truth in your lies.

D5   D5/E   G5   Bm7   Asus4   G5
When everything feels like the movies, yeah, you bleed just to know you're alive.

REPEAT CHORUS

INTERLUDE

‖: Bm7 | Bm7/C♯ | D5 | |

Bm7 | Asus4 | Gmaj7 | :‖

REPEAT CHORUS (2 TIMES)

OUTRO

        Bm7   **Asus4**   **G5**
I just want you to know who I am.

        Bm7   **Asus4**   **G5**
I just want you to know who I am.

        Bm7   **Asus4**   **Bm7**
I just want you to know who I am.

REPEAT INTERLUDE (REPEAT AND FADE)

Knockin' on Heaven's Door

Words and Music by Bob Dylan

 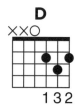 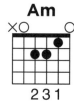 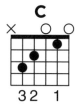

INTRO

Slow

G	D	Am		G	D	C	
Ooh.				Ooh.			

VERSE 1

G　　　　　　**D**　　　　**Am**
Mama, take this　　badge off of me.

G　　　　**D**　　**C**
I can't use　　it anymore.

G　　　　　　**D**　　　　**Am**
It's gettin' dark,　　too dark to see.

G　　　　　　**D**　　　　　**C**
I feel I'm knock - in' on heaven's door.

CHORUS

G　　　　　　**D**　　　　　**Am**
Knock, knock, knockin' on heaven's door.

G　　　　　　**D**　　　　　**C**
Knock, knock, knockin' on heaven's door.

G　　　　　　**D**　　　　　**Am**
Knock, knock, knockin' on heaven's door.

G　　　　　　**D**　　　　　**C**
Knock, knock, knockin' on heaven's door.

VERSE 2

G   D   Am
Mama, put my   guns in the ground.

G   D   C
I can't shoot   them anymore.

G   D   Am
That long, black   cloud is comin' down.

G   D   C
I feel I'm knock - in' on heaven's door.

REPEAT CHORUS

REPEAT INTRO (FADE OUT)

Let Her Go

Words and Music by Michael David Rosenberg

(Capo 7th Fret)

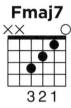 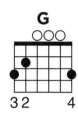  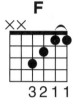 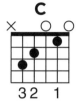 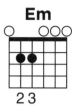

INTRO

Slow

‖: **Fmaj7**   **G** | **Am**   **G** | **Fmaj7**   **G** | **Am**   **G** :‖

CHORUS 1

      G   **F**   **C**   **G**   **Am**
Well, you only need the light when it's burnin' low.   Only miss the sun when it starts to snow.

           F   **C**   **G**
Only know you love her when you let her go.

           F   **C**   **G**   **Am**
Only know you've been high when you're feelin' low.   Only hate the road when you're missin' home.

           F   **C**   **G**
Only know you love her when you let her go.   And you let her go.

INTERLUDE

Am   **Fmaj7** | **G**   **Em** | **Am**   **Fmaj7** | **G**   ‖

VERSE 1

Am   **Fmaj7** **G**   **Em**
Starin' at the bottom of your glass, hoping one day you'll make a dream last.

          Am   **Fmaj7**   **G**
But dreams come slow, and they go so fast.

         Am   **Fmaj7**   **G**   **Em**
You see her when you close your eyes. Maybe one day you'll understand why

          Am   **Fmaj7**   **G**
everything you touch surely dies.

CHORUS 2

G   F   C   G   Am
But you only need the light when it's burnin' low. Only miss the sun when it starts to snow.

       F   C   G
Only know you love her when you let her go.

       F   C   G   Am
Only know you've been high when you're feelin' low. Only hate the road when you're missin' home.

       F   C   G
Only know you love her when you let her go.

VERSE 2

Am   Fmaj7   G   Em
Starin' at the ceilin' in the dark. Same old empty feeling in your heart

      Am   Fmaj7   G
'cause love comes slow, and it goes so fast.

     Am   Fmaj7   G   Em
Well, you see her when you fall asleep. But never to touch and never to keep

       Am   Fmaj7   G
'cause you loved her too much, and you dived too deep.

REPEAT CHORUS 1

BRIDGE

Am Fmaj7 G   Am Fmaj7 G
Oh, oh, oh, no. And you let her go. Oh, oh, oh, no. Well, you let her go.

REPEAT INTERLUDE

REPEAT CHORUS 2

CHORUS 3

      G   F   C   G   Am
'Cause you only need the light when it's burnin' low. Only miss the sun when it starts to snow.

       F   C   G
Only know you love her when you let her go.

N.C.
    Only know you've been high when you're feelin' low. Only hate the road when you're missin' home.

Only know you love her when you let her go.   And you let her go.

Losing My Religion

Words and Music by William Berry, Peter Buck, Michael Mills and Michael Stipe

F	Dm7	G	Am	Em	Dm	C
	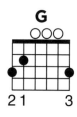	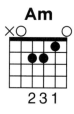				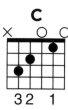
3 2 1 1	2 1 1	2 1 3	2 3 1	1 2	2 3 1	3 2 1

INTRO

Moderately fast

| F | | Dm7   G | Am | | |
| | | | | | |

| F | | Dm7   G | Am | G | |
| | | | | Oh, | |

VERSE 1

Am   Em   Am
life is bigger, it's bigger than you, and you are not me.

        Em   Am
The lengths that I will go to. The distance in your eyes.

Em   Dm   G
 Oh, no, I've said too much. I set it up.

       Am   Em   Am
That's me in the corner. That's me in the spotlight, losin' my religion

    Em   Am
tryin' to keep up with you. And I don't know if I can do it.

Em   Dm   G
 Oh, no, I've said too much. I haven't said enough.

CHORUS 1

         F   Dm7 G Am
I thought that I heard you laughing. I thought that I heard you sing.

 F   Dm7 G Am   G
I think I thought I saw you try.

VERSE 2

    Am   Em   Am
Every whisper of every waking hour I'm choosin' my confessions,

   Em   Am
tryin' to keep an eye on you like a hurt, lost and blinded fool, fool.

Em   Dm   G
 Oh, no, I've said too much. I set it up.

Am   **Em**
Consider this. Consider this the hint of the century.

Am   **Em**
Consider this the slip that brought me to my knees, failed.

Am   **Dm**   **G**
What if all these fantasies come flailing around? Now I've said too much.

REPEAT CHORUS 1

BRIDGE

Am   **G**   **F**   **G**
                                                                                                            But

C   **Dm7**   **C**   **Dm7**
that was just a dream. That was just a dream.

VERSE 3

                       Am   **Em**   **Am**
That's me in the corner. That's me in the spotlight, losin' my religion

         Em   **Am**
tryin' to keep up with you. And I don't know if I can do it.

Em   **Dm**   **G**
   Oh, no, I've said too much. I haven't said enough.

CHORUS 2

                          F   **Dm7**   **G**   **Am**
I thought that I heard you laughing. I thought   that I heard you sing.

F   **Dm7** **G**   **Am**
I think I thought I saw   you   try.

 F   **Dm7**   **G**   **Am**
But that was just a dream.   Try, cry. Why try?

F   **Dm7** **G** **Am**   **G**
That was just a dream,   just a dream, just a dream, dream.

OUTRO

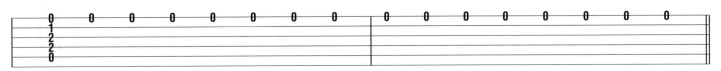

Play 5 times

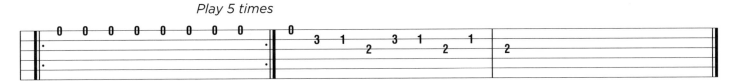

Mr. Jones

Words and Music by Adam Duritz, David Bryson, Charles Gillingham, Matthew Malley,
Steve Bowman, Daniel Vickrey and Ben Mize

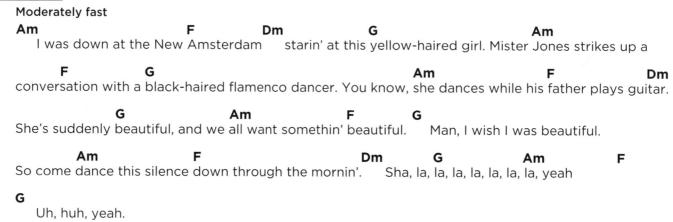

VERSE 1

Moderately fast

Am		F	Dm	G		Am		

I was down at the New Amsterdam   starin' at this yellow-haired girl. Mister Jones strikes up a

F   G   Am   F   Dm

conversation with a black-haired flamenco dancer. You know, she dances while his father plays guitar.

    G   Am   F   G

She's suddenly beautiful, and we all want somethin' beautiful.   Man, I wish I was beautiful.

    Am   F   Dm   G   Am   F

So come dance this silence down through the mornin'.   Sha, la, la, la, la, la, la, la, yeah

G

Uh, huh, yeah.

VERSE 2

Am   F   Dm   G   Am   F   G

Cut up, Maria!   Show me some of them Spanish dances, and   pass me a bottle, Mister Jones.

Am   F   Dm   G   Am   F   G

Believe in me.   Help me believe in anything 'cause I want to be someone who believes,   yeah.

CHORUS 1

C   F   G   C   F

Mister Jones and me   tell each other fairy tales, and we   stare at the beautiful women.

    G   C   F

"She's lookin' at you. Ah, no, no, she's lookin' at me." Smilin' in the bright lights,

G   C   F   G

comin' through in stereo. When everybody loves   you,   you can never be lonely.

VERSE 3

    Am   F   Dm   G   Am

Well, I'm gonna paint my picture,   paint myself in blue and red and black and gray.   All of the

F   G   Am   F

beautiful colors are very, very   meaningful. Yeah, well, you know, gray is my favorite color. I

Dm   G   Am   F   G

felt so symbolic yesterday.   If I knew Picasso, I would buy myself a gray guitar and play.

CHORUS 2

C   F   G   C   F
Mister Jones and me   look into the future, yeah, we   stare at the beautiful women.

         G   C   F
"She's lookin' at you. I don't think so, she's lookin' at me." Standin' in the spotlight,

G   C   F   G
I bought myself a gray guitar. When everybody loves   me,   I will never be lonely.

BRIDGE

Am   Fmaj7   Am   G Am   Fmaj7
I will never be lone - ly. Said I'm never gonna be lone - ly.   I want to be a lion. Eh, everybody

                     Am   G
want to pass as cats.   We all want to be big, big stars, yeah, but   we got different reasons for that.

Am   Fmaj7   Am
Believe in me 'cause I don't believe in anything, and I,   I want to be someone to believe,

G
to believe, to believe, yeah.

CHORUS 3

C   F   G   C   F
Mister Jones and me   stumblin' through the barrio, yeah, we   stare at the beautiful women.

         G   C   F
"She's perfect for you. Man, there's got to be somebody for me." I wanna be Bob Dylan. Mister Jones

G   C   F
wishes he was someone just a little more funky. When everybody loves you, aw, son,

G
that's just about as funky as you can be.

CHORUS 4

C   F   G   C   F   G
Mister Jones and me   starin' at the video, when I look at the television, I want to see me

                        C   F   G
starin' right back at me.   We all want to be big stars, but we don't know why, and we don't know how.

               C   F   G
But when everybody loves   me, I'm gonna be   just about as happy as I can be.

OUTRO

C   F   G
Mister Jones and me   we're gonna be big stars.

More Than Words

Words and Music by Nuno Bettencourt and Gary Cherone

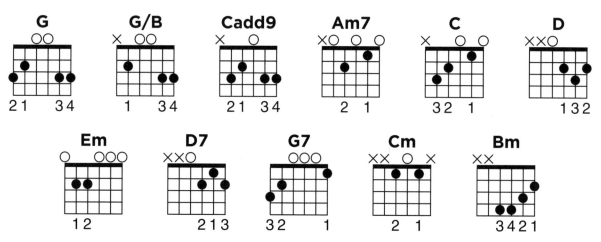

INTRO

Moderately

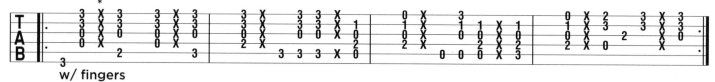

w/ fingers

*Slap muted strings w/ right hand throughout.

VERSE 1

G	G/B	Cadd9	Am7		C	D	G

Sayin', "I love you," is not the words I want to hear from you.

	G/B	Cadd9	Am7		C	D	Em		Am7

It's not that I want you not to say, but if you only knew how easy

D7		G	D	Em

it would be to show me how you feel.

CHORUS 1

	Am7	D7		G7		C

More than words is all you have to do to make it real.

	Cm		G		Em		Am7 D7	G

Then you wouldn't have to say that you love me 'cause I'd al - ready know.

	D	Em	Bm	C

What would you do if my heart was torn in two?

	Am7		D7		G

More than words to show you feel that your love for me is real.

	D	Em	Bm	C

What would you say if I took those words away?

	Am7		D7

Then you couldn't make things new just by say - in', "I love

INTERLUDE

G	G/B		Cadd9		Am7		C	D
you."			La, dee, da, la, dee,		da, dee, dai, dai,		da.	More than

G	G/B		Cadd9		Am7	D7		
words.			La, dee, da, dai,		da.			‖

VERSE 2

G   G/B   Cadd9 Am7   C   D   G
Now that I've tried to talk to you and make you under - stand,

G/B   Cadd9   Am7   C   D   Em   Am7
all you have to do is close your eyes and just reach out your hands, and touch me.

D7   G   D   Em
Hold me close, don't ever let me go.

CHORUS 2

         Am7   D7   G7   C
More than words is all I ever needed you to show.

         Cm   G   Em   Am7 D7   G
Then you wouldn't have to say that you love me 'cause I'd al - ready know.

         D   Em   Bm   C
What would you do if my heart was torn in two?

         Am7   D7   G
More than words to show you feel that your love for me is real.

         D   Em   Bm   C
What would you say if I took those words away?

         Am7   D7
Then you couldn't make things new just by say - in', "I love

OUTRO

G	G/B		Cadd9		Am7		C	D
you."			La, dee, da, la, dee,		da, dee, dai, dai,		da.	More than

G	G/B		Cadd9		Am7		C	D
words.			La, dee, da, dai,		da, dee, dai, dai,		da.	More than

G	G/B		Cadd9		Am7		C	D
words.			La, dee, da, dai,		da, dee, dai, dai,		da.	More than

G	G/B		Cadd9		Am7		C	D
words.			La, dee, da, dai,		da.		La, da, da.	More than

G	
words.	‖

Photograph

Words and Music by Ed Sheeran, Johnny McDaid,
Martin Peter Harrington and Tom Leonard

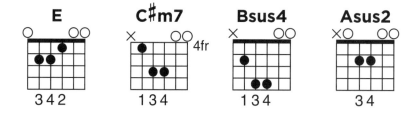

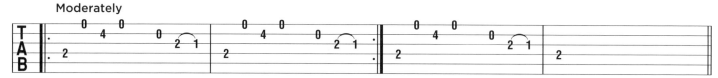

INTRO

Moderately

Play 3 times

VERSE 1

        E   C#m7
Loving can hurt, loving can hurt sometimes,

      Bsus4   Asus2
but it's the only thing that I know.

           E   C#m7
And when it gets hard, you know it can get hard sometimes.

      Bsus4   Asus2
It is the only thing that makes us feel alive.

PRE-CHORUS

C#m7   Asus2   E
   We keep this love in a photograph,   we made these memories for ourselves. Where our

C#m7   Asus2   E   Bsus4
eyes are never closin', hearts are never broken, and time's forever frozen still.

CHORUS 1

          E   Bsus4
So you can keep me inside the pocket of your ripped jeans, holdin' me closer

      C#m7   Asus2   E
till our eyes meet. You won't ever be alone. Wait for me to come home.

VERSE 2

N.C.   E   C#m7
Loving can heal, loving can mend your soul,

        Bsus4   Asus2
and it's the only thing that I know, know.

           E   C#m7
I swear it will get easier, remember that with every piece of you.

        Bsus4   Asus2
Mm, and it's the only thing we take with us when we die.

REPEAT PRE-CHORUS

CHORUS 2

       E   Bsus4
So you can keep me inside the pocket of your ripped jeans, holdin' me closer

   C#m7   Asus2
till our eyes meet. You won't ever be alone.

       E   Bsus4
And if you hurt me, well that's ok, baby, only words bleed inside these pages.

   C#m7   Asus2
You just hold me. I won't ever let you go.

BRIDGE

         C#m7   Asus2
Wait for me to come home. Wait for me to come home.

         E   Bsus4
Wait for me to come home. Wait for me to come home, ooh.

CHORUS 3

       E   Bsus4
Oh, you can fit me inside the necklace you got when you were sixteen, next to your heartbeat

   C#m7   Asus2
where I should be. Keep it deep within your soul.

       E   Bsus4
And if you hurt me, well that's ok, baby, only words bleed inside these pages.

   C#m7   Asus2
You just hold me. I won't ever let you go.

OUTRO

       E   Bsus4
And when I'm away, I will remember how you kissed me under the lamppost

   C#m7   Asus2   N.C.
back on Sixth Street, hearing you whisper through the phone. Wait for me to come home.

Riptide

Words and Music by Vance Joy

(Capo 1st Fret)

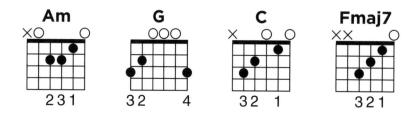

INTRO

Moderately slow

‖: Am   G | C   :‖

VERSE 1

Am   G   C   Am   G   C
I was scared of dentists and the dark.   I was scared of pretty girls and starting conversations.

Am   G   C   Am   G   C
Oh, all my friends   are turnin' green. You're the magician's assistant in their dream. Ah,

PRE-CHORUS

Am   G   C   Am   G   C
ooh. | | Oh,   and they | come unstuck.   ‖

CHORUS 1

Am   G   C   Am   G   C
Lady, runnin' down to the riptide, taken away to the dark side. I wanna be your left-hand man.

Am   G   C
I love you when you're singin' that song, and I got a lump in my

Am   G   C
throat 'cause you're gonna sing the words   wrong.

VERSE 2

Am   G   C   Am   G   C
Here's this movie that I think you'll like. This guy decides to quit his job and heads to New York City.

Am   G   C   Am   G   C
This cowboy's runnin' from himself, and she's been livin' on the highest shelf. Ah,

REPEAT PRE-CHORUS

REPEAT CHORUS 1

INTERLUDE

C | ‖

BRIDGE

Am   G   C   Fmaj7
I just wanna, I just wanna know   if you're gonna, if you're gonna stay.

Am   G   C   Fmaj7
I just gotta, I just gotta know.   I can't have it, I can't have it any other way.

 Am   G   C   Am   G   C
I swear she's destined for the screen.   Closest thing to Michelle Pfeiffer that you've ever seen, oh.

REPEAT CHORUS 1 (2 TIMES)

CHORUS 2

Am G   C   Am   G   C
Lady, runnin' down to the riptide, taken away to the dark side. I wanna be your left-hand man.

 Am   G   C   .
I love you when you're singin' that song, and I got a lump in my

Am   G   C
throat 'cause you're gonna sing the words wrong, yeah. I got a lump in my

Am   G   C
throat 'cause you're gonna sing the words   wrong.

The Scientist

Words and Music by Guy Berryman, Jon Buckland, Will Champion and Chris Martin

(Capo 1st Fret)

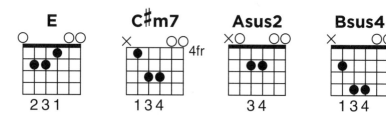

INTRO

Slow

E | ‖

VERSE 1

C#m7   Asus2   E
Come up to meet you, tell you I'm sor - ry, you don't know how lovely you are.

C#m7 Asus2   E
I had to find you, tell you I need you, tell you I'll set you apart.

C#m7   Asus2   E
So, tell me your se - crets, and ask me your ques - tions, oh, let's go back to the start.

C#m7 Asus2   E
Runnin' in cir - cles, comin' up tails, heads on a science apart.

CHORUS 1

Asus2   E
Nobody said it was easy, oh, it's such a shame for us to part.

Asus2   E   Bsus4
Nobody said it was easy, no one ever said it would be this hard. I'm goin' back to the start.

INTERLUDE 1

E | Asus2 | E | ‖

VERSE 2

C#m7   Asus2   E
And I was just gues - sin' at numbers and fig - ures, pullin' your puzzles apart.

C#m7 Asus2   E
Questions of sci - ence, science and pro - gress do not speak as loud as my heart.

C#m7   Asus2   E
So tell me you love me, or come back and haunt me, oh, when I rush to the start.

C#m7   Asus2   E
Runnin' in cir - cles, chasin' our tails, comin' back as we are.

CHORUS 2

Asus2   **E**
 Nobody said it was easy, oh, it's such a shame for us to part.

Asus2   **E**   **Bsus4**
 Nobody said it was easy, no one ever said it would be so hard. Oh, take me back to the start.

INTERLUDE 2

E		**Asus2**		**E**				
C♯m7		**Asus2**		**E**				

OUTRO

Play 3 times

‖: **C♯m7** | **Asus2** | **E** | | :‖
  Ah, ooh, ooh, ooh, ooh, ooh.

C♯m7 | **Asus2** | **E** | ‖
  Ah, ooh, ooh, ooh, ooh, ooh.

Tears in Heaven

Words and Music by Eric Clapton and Will Jennings

(Capo 2nd Fret)

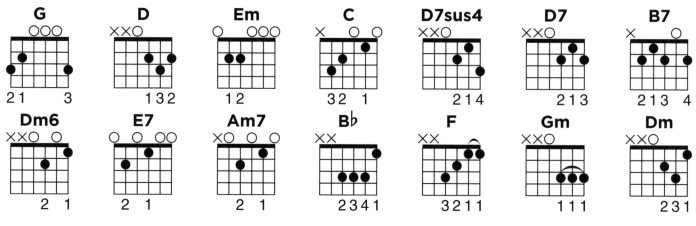

INTRO

Moderately slow

| G | D | Em   G | C   D7sus4 D7 | G | ‖

VERSE 1

G   D Em   G   C   G   D
Would you know my name   if I saw you in heaven?

G   D Em   G   C   G   D
Would it be the same   if I saw you in heaven?

CHORUS 1

Em   B7   Dm6   E7   Am7   D7sus4   G
I must be strong   and carry on 'cause I know I don't belong here in heaven.

REPEAT INTRO

VERSE 2

G   D Em   G   C   G   D
Would you hold my hand   if I saw you in heaven?

G   D Em   G   C   G   D
Would you help me stand   if I saw you in heaven?

CHORUS 2

Em   B7   Dm6   E7   Am7   D7sus4   G
I'll find my way   through night and day 'cause I know I just can't stay here in heaven.

REPEAT INTRO

BRIDGE

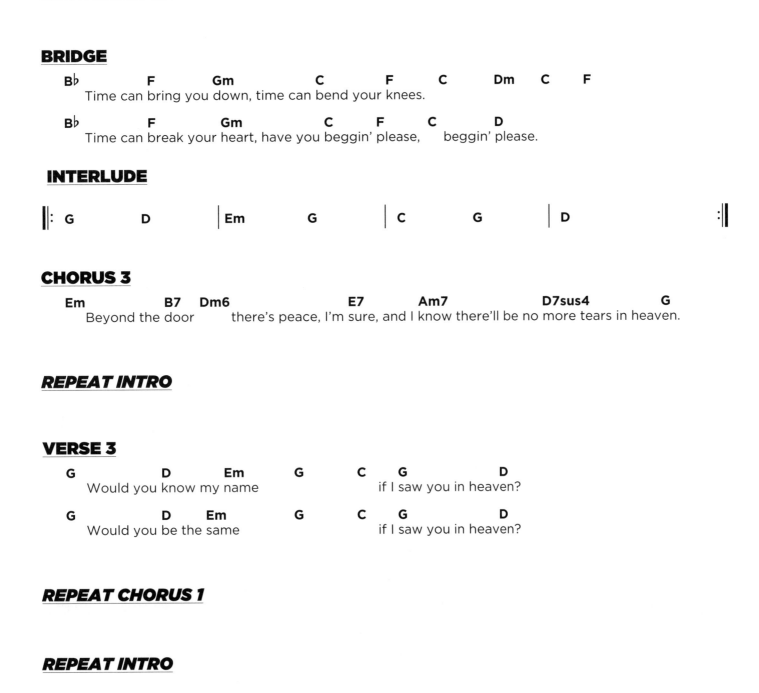

B♭   F   Gm   C   F   C   Dm C   F
    Time can bring you down, time can bend your knees.

B♭   F   Gm   C   F   C   D
    Time can break your heart, have you beggin' please,   beggin' please.

INTERLUDE

‖: G   D | Em   G | C   G | D   :‖

CHORUS 3

Em   B7   Dm6   E7   Am7   D7sus4   G
    Beyond the door   there's peace, I'm sure, and I know there'll be no more tears in heaven.

REPEAT INTRO

VERSE 3

G   D   Em   G   C   G   D
Would you know my name   if I saw you in heaven?

G   D   Em   G   C   G   D
Would you be the same   if I saw you in heaven?

REPEAT CHORUS 1

REPEAT INTRO

Wagon Wheel

Words and Music by Bob Dylan and Ketch Secor

(Capo 2nd Fret)

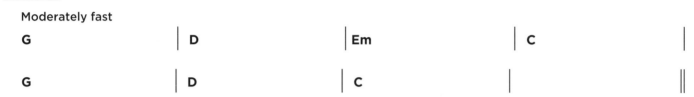

INTRO

Moderately fast

| G | | D | | Em | | C | | | |
| G | | D | | C | | | | | |

VERSE 1

G   D   Em   C
Headin' down south to the land of the pines, I'm thumbin' my way into North Carolina,

G   D   C
starin' up the road and pray to God I see headlights.

G   D   Em   C
I made it down the coast in seventeen hours pickin' me a bouquet of dogwood flowers, and I'm

G   D   C
hopin' for Raleigh, I can see my baby tonight.

CHORUS

G   D   Em   C
So, rock me, mama, like a wagon wheel. Rock me, mama, any way you feel.

G D   C
Hey,   mama, rock me.

G   D   Em   C
Rock me, mama, like the wind and rain. Rock me, mama, like a south-bound train.

G D   C
Hey,   mama, rock me.

REPEAT INTRO

VERSE 2

    G   D   Em   C
I'm runnin' from the cold up in New England. I was born to be a fiddler in an old-time string band.

    G   D   C
My baby plays the guitar,   I pick a banjo now.

    G   D   Em   C
Oh, north country winters keep gettin' me down, lost my money playin' poker so I had to leave town.

    G   D   C
But I ain't turnin' back to livin' that old life no more.

REPEAT CHORUS

REPEAT INTRO

VERSE 3

G   D   Em   C
Walkin' to the south outta Roanoke, I caught a trucker outta Philly, had a nice long toke.

    G   D   C
But he's headin' west from the Cumberland Gap to Johnson City, Tennessee.

    G   D   Em   C
I gotta get a move on before the sun. I hear my baby callin' my name, and I know that she's the only one.

    G   D   C
And if I die in Raleigh, at least I will die   free.

REPEAT CHORUS (2 TIMES)

REPEAT INTRO (REPEAT AND FADE)

What I Got

Words and Music by Brad Nowell, Eric Wilson, Floyd Gaugh and Lindon Roberts

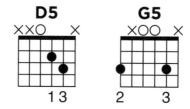

INTRO

Moderately slow

| D5 | G5 | D5 | G5 | |

VERSE 1

D5 G5 D5 G5
Early in the mornin', risin' to the street.

D5 G5 D5 G5
Light me up that cigarette, and I strap shoes on my feet.

D5 G5 D5 G5
Got to find a reason, reason things went wrong.

D5 G5 D5 G5
Got to find a reason why my money's all gone.

D5 G5 D5 G5
I got a Dalmation, and I can still get high.

D5 G5 D5 G5
I can play the guitar like a motherfuckin' riot.

REPEAT INTRO (2 TIMES)

VERSE 2

D5 G5 D5 G5
Well, life is too short, so love the one you got 'cause you might get run over or you might get shot.

D5 G5 D5 G5
Never start no static, I just get it off my chest. Never had to battle with no bulletproof vest.

D5 G5 D5 G5
Take a small example, take a ti, ti, ti, tip from me. Take all of your money, give it all to charity.

| D5 | | G5 | | D5 | | G5 |
Love is what I got. It's within my reach, and the Sublime style's still straight from Long Beach. It all

| D5 | | G5 | | D5 | | G5 |
comes back to you. You finally get what you deserve. Try and test that, you're bound to get served.

| D5 | | G5 | | D5 | | G5 |
Love's what I got. Don't start a riot. You feel it when the dance gets hot.

CHORUS

D5 G5 D5 G5
Lovin'   is what I got. I said remember that.

D5 G5 D5 G5
Lovin'   is what I got, and remember that.

D5 G5 D5 G5
Lovin'   is what I got. I said remember that.

D5 G5 D5 G5
Lovin'   is what I got, I got, I got, I got.

VERSE 3

D5 G5 D5 G5
Why, I don't cry when my dog runs away.   I don't get angry at the bills I have to pay.

D5 G5 D5 G5
I don't get angry when my mom smokes pot,   hits the bottle and goes right to the rock.

D5 G5 D5 G5
Fuckin' and fightin', it's all the same. Livin' with Louie Dog's the only way to stay sane.

D5 G5 D5
Let the lovin', let the lovin' come back to me.

INTERLUDE

‖: D5   G5 | D5   G5 :‖ D5 | 'Cause ‖

REPEAT CHORUS

REPEAT INTRO (REPEAT AND FADE)

Wonderwall

Words and Music by Noel Gallagher

(Capo 2nd Fret)

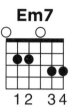 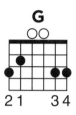  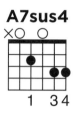 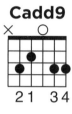 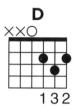

INTRO

Moderately

$\|$: Em7   G | Dsus4   A7sus4 | Em7   G | Dsus4   A7sus4   :$\|$

VERSE 1

Em7   G   Dsus4   A7sus4
Today is gonna be the day that they're gonna throw it back to you.

Em7   G   Dsus4   A7sus4
By now, you should have somehow realized what you gotta do.

Em7   G   Dsus4   A7sus4
I don't believe that anybody feels the way I do about you now.

Cadd9   Dsus4 | A7sus4 $\|$

VERSE 2

Em7   G   Dsus4   A7sus4
Backbeat, the word is on the street that the fire in your heart is out.

Em7   G   Dsus4   A7sus4
I'm sure you've heard it all before, but you never really had a doubt.

Em7   G   Dsus4   A7sus4
I don't believe that anybody feels the way I do about you now.

Em7   G | Dsus4   A7sus4 $\|$

PRE-CHORUS 1

Cadd9   D   Em7
And all the roads we have to walk are winding.

Cadd9   D   Em7
And all the lights that lead us there are blinding.

Cadd9   D   G   D   Em7   G   A7sus4
There are many things that I would like to say to you, but I don't know how.   Because

CHORUS 1

Cadd9 **Em7** **G** **Em7**
maybe you're gonna be the one that

Cadd9 **Em7** **G** **Em7**
saves me. and after

Cadd9 **Em7** **G** **Em7**
all you're my wonder -

Cadd9 **Em7** **G** **Em7**
wall. *(2nd and 3rd times)* I said,

VERSE 3

Em7 **G** **Dsus4** **A7sus4**
Today was gonna be the day, but they'll never throw it back to you.

Em7 **G** **Dsus4** **A7sus4**
By now, you should have somehow realized what you're not to do.

Em7 **G** **Dsus4** **A7sus4**
I don't believe that anybody feels the way I do about you now.

Em7 **G** | **Dsus4** **A7sus4** ‖

PRE-CHORUS 2

Cadd9 **D** **Em7**
And all the roads that lead you there were winding.

Cadd9 **D** **Em7**
And all the lights that light the way are blinding.

Cadd9 **D** **G** **D** **Em7** **G** **A7sus4**
There are many things that I would like to say to you, but I don't know how. I said,

REPEAT CHORUS 1 (2 TIMES)

CHORUS 2

Cadd9 **Em7** **G** **Em7**
maybe you're gonna be the one that

Cadd9 **Em7** **G** **Em7**
saves me. You're gonna be the one that

Cadd9 **Em7** **G** **Em7**
saves me. You're gonna be the one that

Cadd9 **Em7** **G** **Em7**
saves me.

OUTRO

‖: **Cadd9** **Em7** | **G** **Em7** | **Cadd9** **Em7** | **G** **Em7** :‖

Guitar Chord Songbooks

Each 6" x 9" book includes complete lyrics, chord symbols, and guitar chord diagrams.

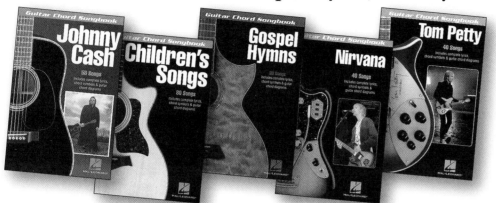

Acoustic Hits
00701787 . . . . $14.99
Acoustic Rock
00699540 . . . . $22.99
Alabama
00699914 . . . . $14.95
The Beach Boys
00699566 . . . . $19.99
Bluegrass
00702585 . . . . $14.99
Johnny Cash
00699648 . . . . $19.99
Children's Songs
00699539 . . . . $17.99
Christmas Carols
00699536 . . . . $14.99
Christmas Songs
00119911 . . . . $14.99
Eric Clapton
00699567 . . . . $19.99
Classic Rock
00699598 . . . . $20.99
Coffeehouse Hits
00703318 . . . . $14.99
Country
00699534 . . . . $17.99
Country Favorites
00700609 . . . . $14.99
Country Hits
00140859 . . . . $14.99
Country Standards
00700608 . . . . $12.95
Cowboy Songs
00699636 . . . . $19.99
Creedence Clearwater Revival
00701786 . . . . $16.99
Jim Croce
00148087 . . . . $14.99
Crosby, Stills & Nash
00701609 . . . . $17.99
John Denver
02501697 . . . . $19.99
Neil Diamond
00700606 . . . . $22.99
Disney – 2nd Edition
00295786 . . . . $19.99

The Doors
00699888 . . . . $22.99
Eagles
00122917 . . . . $19.99
Early Rock
00699916 . . . . $14.99
Folksongs
00699541 . . . . $16.99
Folk Pop Rock
00699651 . . . . $17.99
40 Easy Strumming Songs
00115972 . . . . $16.99
Four Chord Songs
00701611 . . . . $16.99
Glee
00702501 . . . . $14.99
Gospel Hymns
00700463 . . . . $16.99
Grateful Dead
00139461 . . . . $17.99
Green Day
00103074 . . . . $17.99
Irish Songs
00701044 . . . . $16.99
Michael Jackson
00137847 . . . . $14.99
Billy Joel
00699632 . . . . $22.99
Elton John
00699732 . . . . $17.99
Ray LaMontagne
00130337 . . . . $12.99
Latin Songs
00700973 . . . . $14.99
Love Songs
00701043 . . . . $14.99
Bob Marley
00701704 . . . . $17.99
Bruno Mars
00125332 . . . . $12.99
Paul McCartney
00385035 . . . . $19.99

Steve Miller
00701146 . . . . $12.99
Modern Worship
00701801 . . . . $19.99
Motown
00699734 . . . . $19.99
Willie Nelson
00148273 . . . . $17.99
Nirvana
00699762 . . . . $17.99
Roy Orbison
00699752 . . . . $19.99
Peter, Paul & Mary
00103013 . . . . $19.99
Tom Petty
00699883 . . . . $17.99
Pink Floyd
00139116 . . . . $17.99
Pop/Rock
00699538 . . . . $19.99
Praise & Worship
00699634 . . . . $14.99
Elvis Presley
00699633 . . . . $17.99
Queen
00702395 . . . . $17.99
Red Hot Chili Peppers
00699710 . . . . $24.99
The Rolling Stones
00137716 . . . . $19.99
Bob Seger
00701147 . . . . $16.99
Carly Simon
00121011 . . . . $14.99
Sting
00699921 . . . . $24.99
Three Chord Acoustic Songs
00123860 . . . . $16.99
Three Chord Songs
00699720 . . . . $17.99
Two-Chord Songs
00119236 . . . . $16.99
U2
00137744 . . . . $19.99
Hank Williams
00700607 . . . . $16.99
Stevie Wonder
00120862 . . . . $14.99

Prices and availability subject to change without notice.

Visit Hal Leonard online at **www.halleonard.com**